Good
Morning,
Good
GOD!

D0981245

Good Morning, Good GOD!

Fr. Austin Fleming
"The Concord Pastor"

Copyright © 2016 by Austin Fleming
All rights reserved.

Published by The Word Among Us Press
7115 Guilford Drive, Suite 100
Frederick, Maryland 21704
www.wau.org

21 20 19 18 17   2 3 4 5 6

ISBN: 978-1-59325-279-3
eISBN: 978-1-59325-481-0

Unless otherwise noted, Scripture texts are paraphrased by the author.

Cover design by Koechel Peterson & Associates

No part of this publication may be reproduced, stored in a retrieval
system, or transmitted in any form or by any means—electronic,
mechanical, photocopy, recording, or any other—except for brief
quotations in printed reviews, without the prior permission of the
author and publisher.

Made and printed in the United States of America

Library of Congress Control Number: 2015957596

Contents

Holidays...185

INTRODUCTION

This work began eight years ago. I was a regular reader of several Catholic blogs and often mused about becoming a blogger myself. Doubting that I had the technical savvy required, I let it remain just a thought for some time. That all changed on a rainy day in July 2007. It was my day off and I had nothing planned, so I searched the Internet for information and soon discovered that setting up a blog was very easy. By the end of the afternoon, *A Concord Pastor Comments* was online!

In the early days I wrote on prayer, spirituality, liturgy, and various other Catholic topics. One of my early features was a weekly post entitled "Monday Morning Offering."

The response to this was very good, and it encouraged me to begin writing more prayers for my blog. Over the years I turned my attention primarily to prayer and spirituality, with weekly attention to the Sunday Scriptures.

I'm often asked how much time it takes for me to post daily prayers. On some days the post seems to write itself, while on other days more time is needed. Posting daily prayers has become part of my ministry, and I find great joy in doing it. That my readers find some spiritual nourishment in this work is a blessing. Especially gratifying is to hear from so many readers who tell me that they've forwarded a particular prayer post to others whom they believed would benefit from it. The word spreads with the help of my readership as much as with the help of Facebook and Twitter!

My aim is to write prayers that touch on the ups and downs, the hopes and fears, of a broad spectrum of people. I also try to write in language accessible to people at many different stages in the spiritual life, novice to master. My goal is to phrase my prayers in a vocabulary known and spoken by many hearts. It's a grace for me when readers tell me that my words spoke just what they were trying to bring to speech in their own prayer. When this happens, I'm confident that the Lord is involved in the process.

My daily posts are also part of my own prayer life. Some posts, but certainly not all of them, reflect what's happening in my own heart and spiritual life. Some posts come from the milieu of my parish ministry and my sharing in the prayers, joys, and sorrows of so many. Choosing a direction for each day's prayer is under the guidance of the Holy Spirit, whose help I rely on all the time!

I'm very pleased that *The Word Among Us Press* is publishing this collection of prayers from my blog, and I'm pleased to share these with a new and wider readership. I pray that these words will nourish your spiritual life and that you might pass them on to others who might find in them a help to their own prayer.

Fr. Austin Fleming

Will You Join Me Today, Lord?

O God, it's morning!

And once again, you're up before I am.
It never fails: I turn off the alarm clock
and there you are, sitting at the foot of my bed,
waiting, watching, wanting to be
the first thought of my day.

Please forgive me, Lord,
but most days I don't *have* a first thought
until I've had my first cup of coffee.
So, please, be patient with me,
as you always are,
and give me time to wake
to your presence.

I'm wondering, Lord . . .
Where am I going today?
Where will you lead me?
What path will you light for me?

Please, Lord, when I walk astray
or try to take the shortcut,
prod me, pull me, push me back
where I belong, where I should be heading,

even should that path be the one
I'm least inclined to walk.

Take me down the just path, Lord;
lead me on the road to truth;
guide me down the highway of honesty;
give me strength to walk with proper pride
in the ways of integrity.

Help me to see that the only path worth walking
is the one that leads me to you
and to love and serve my neighbor.

It's morning, Lord!
I'm getting up now to have that cup of coffee.

Will you join me? Amen.

Saving a Place for You

I will not enter the house where I live,
nor go to the bed where I rest.
I will give no sleep to my eyes,
to my eyelids I will give no slumber
till I find a place for the LORD.
—Psalm 132:3-5

What place in my life have I found for you, Lord?
What part of my day do I set aside to be with you,
to sit and talk with you?

Do I have a place for you in all the things I do
each morning as I get ready to face the day?
Do I save a seat for you on the train or in my car
as I go to work?
When I'm home alone for the day,
do I invite you to share my morning coffee?

Have I a place for you in my heart
with all its hurts and burdens, its hopes and joys?
Have I a place in my mind for your word,
your truth, your wisdom?

Do I find a place for you at the end of my day,
in prayer, as my eyes grow heavy
and I lay me down to sleep?

I know you have a place in your day for me, Lord.
I know you have a place in your heart
for me to rest my weary soul and find some peace.
I know you're never too busy to find a time and place
to sit with me . . . to be with me.
to listen to me . . . to speak to me.

Help me find a place today, Lord;
help me find and make a place for you.
Amen.

YOUR LIGHT SHINES THROUGH

No matter how high the trees,
no matter how close the branches,
no matter how dense the foliage,
your light shines through, O Lord.

No matter how gray the sky,
no matter how thick the clouds,
no matter how heavy the rains,
your light shines through, O Lord.

No matter how dark the night,
no matter how few the twinkling stars,
no matter how thin the silvery moon,
your light shines through, O Lord.

No matter how dark my path,
no matter how gray my thoughts,
no matter the tears that dim my sight,
your light shines through, O Lord.

No matter the shadows of fear,
no matter the dusk of doubt:
lift my head and my heart to see
how your light shines through on me. Amen.

Someone Else's Day

I could use an easy, happy, peaceful day, Lord.

But before I pray that for myself, open my eyes
to how I might make someone *else's* day
easier, happier, and more peaceful.

How strong is the human spirit
and, at the same time,
how fragile and how vulnerable.

Let my spirit be strong for others today, Lord,
and make me gentle in all I say and do. Amen.

DRAW ME INTO YOUR HEART OF HEARTS

Good morning, good God!

I offer you this morning
the things that get in faith's way in my life.

I offer my disappointment, Lord,
when you don't do what I want you to do
and in the way I want you to do it.
Help me remember
that you are not my servant;
that I am yours.

I offer my impatience, Lord,
when you respond so slowly to my prayers
and the doubts I have,
when you seem not to hear my prayers at all.
Help me trust that you hear every prayer I offer
long before it's in my heart or on my lips.

I offer you my envy, Lord,
when I fret about not having all that others have.
Open my eyes wide to the gifts I do have,
to the blessings I've received,
to the peace and joy

you have in store for me
and want me to find and have.

I offer you my hopelessness, Lord,
when I feel my life is like the wind,
that I shall never see happiness again.
Help me trust, Lord,
that when I cannot find you,
you are still by my side;
that even when I feel abandoned,
you hold me in the palm of your hand.

Draw me from myself, Lord,
and into your heart of hearts.
Help me to welcome you as my Redeemer,
the One whom I shall see with my own eyes,
the One who promises and will bring me peace. Amen.

Light and Color to My Soul

Lord,
Every day you paint millions of landscapes
all around the world:
each one brushed by your careful hand,
each a masterpiece, each unique.

All outdoors is your museum, Lord,
and the entrance fee's no more
than what free time it takes for me to browse
the peaks and valleys of your artistry.

All outdoors, Lord:
from mountaintops to plains and deserts;
from canyons grand to shore lines long;
from the far away to the sidewalk passing
right by my front door.

I needn't travel far to find your work:
your presence and your beauty
breathe and bloom on every side,
in everything around me.

As I come and go today, Lord,
let my eyes not miss your masterpieces
all along my path:
from the sidewalk passing by my door
to wherever on this day
your Spirit leads me. Amen.

My Wise and Gentle Shepherd

Good morning, good God!

I need a shepherd, Lord,
and *you* are the good shepherd
whose voice I listen for,
whose word I want to hear,
whose path I want to follow.

But sometimes I get lost,
and listen as I might,
I find it hard to hear your voice
when I need you most of all.

Good shepherd,
keep me from evil when it nears my path,
and help me to trust
that you are by my side this day,
this night, and always.

Open my eyes and my heart, Lord,
to the ways I might shepherd others
whose paths cross my mine this day, this week.

Be my wise and gentle shepherd, Lord,
and at this day's end, tend my way home
to your flock, your arms, and your peace. Amen.

Trusting in Your Plan

We spend a good deal of our time waiting, hoping, and praying.
We wait for news and pray it will be good.
We wait for healing and pray it will come.
We wait for answers and pray we will understand them.
Here's a prayer for those who wait and hope and pray.

You leave us hanging, Lord,
twixt tomorrow and today,
the known and all unknown,
our fears and all our dreams.

Between what's now and yet to be,
there lies a simple truth:
all is in your hands, O Lord,
while ours fold and hold in prayer our hope.

And we trust you'll lead us from this time
beyond our tears and fears
to peace, O Lord, and trust in you
and in your plan for us.

And if not peace, then faith
to fold our hands again in yours
and hold your strength as ours, O Lord,
and rest within your arms. Amen.

Clean House in My Heart

Let the words of my mouth meet with your favor,
Lord, keep the thoughts of my hearts before you.
—Psalm 19:15

Lord, there are thoughts renting space in my heart,
a place where they've no right to be.

And too many words spill from my lips
before I consider their meaning.

Clean house in my heart and sweep away all
but the thoughts that are pleasing to you.

Place a guard at my lips and govern my speech,
lest I do any harm with my words.

Let the words of my mouth find favor with you, Lord;
let the thoughts of my heart be loving and just. Amen.

Be King of My Life

Be my powerful King, Lord:
give me strength when I am weak
and let your just way be my path.

Keep me from treasuring what has no worth;
protect me when I am afraid;
rescue me from my lack of faith and trust.

Be the light in the darkness of my worry,
the joy in the shadows of my grief,
the ruler of my deeds and desires.

Be the just and gentle King of my life, Lord,
and teach my heart to long to see you
soon and very soon. Amen.

When My Head Is Spinning

Especially when there's too much going on, Lord,
remind me to make time to sit, quietly, with you.

Especially when my head's spinning in confusion,
turn my heart to your word and wisdom.

Especially when it all seems too much to bear,
lift up my soul with your presence and your peace.

Especially today, Lord, please do all of this for me.
Amen.

In Your Company

Good morning, good God!

Sometimes, Lord,
when I look at the day ahead of me
I wonder and worry
how I'm going to make my way to its end.

Sometimes I look at the week or the month ahead
and wonder how I'll get from here to there,
to the other side of what seems immovable,
impassable, impossible.

But day after day, week after week,
I get there, Lord;
no matter how slowly the day,
the week, the month—even the hour—may pass,
I get there.

Looking back on the path I've walked,
so often the journey seems shorter, simpler, safer
than what I imagined at its beginning.

Help me remember, Lord, at this day's start
and as I survey the week and month before me,
help me remember,
when even the next hour seems too much to bear,
help me remember that my passage will be safe,
my burdens lighter,
the length of my day will be halved,
with you in my heart, by my side. Amen.

THE PEOPLE I'LL MEET TODAY

The people I'll meet today
are people with things on their mind,
aches and pains in their bodies,
troubles in their souls,
and hurt in their hearts.

They'll be busy, sad, distracted, and
preoccupied with problems large and small;
they'll be hoping for the day to end
and wondering if it ever will.

In other words, Lord,
the people I'll meet today will be, in many ways,
just like me.

So help me be as gentle, Lord,
as I'd have others be with me.

Help me be patient
when I can't figure out what's bothering them,
let alone what's bothering me.

Help me be forgiving
of what I don't see or know,
remembering how I hide so well
what makes a grouch of me.

Help me help my friends, Lord,
to make it through this day,
and open me to the help you give
when tomorrow seems a year away. Amen.

A Prayer When God Is Silent

Lord,
help me know the silence,
your deep silence,
as a gift.

Help me come into your silence,
and wait there
in the quiet
for your peace.

Help me find within your silence
not the void of absence
but the fullness of your presence.

Help me trust that in your silence
I will find you and we'll meet:
the beloved and the Lover,
in the silence
where every sound is hushed
and love's the only Word.

In your silence, Lord, I am
who I'm truly made to be,
for only in your silence,
in the silence of your Word,
am I truly known and loved.

Help me know you in your silence, Lord,
that I might come to know
who in your love I am
and who I'm called to be. Amen.

I Trust You, Lord

Lord,
I trust in your presence when I feel all alone.
I trust you'll follow me when I walk away.
I trust you'll find me when I get lost.
I trust in your promise when hope has run out.
I trust in your wisdom when my thinking's confused.
I trust you're with me when others have left me.
I trust your compassion when I'm distressed.
I trust in your comfort when I'm deep in grief.
I trust in your strength when I'm weak and afraid.

I trust in your love when I don't love myself.
I trust in your mercy when I've fallen from grace.
I trust in your Spirit when I'm down and out.
I trust in you, Lord, when my trust is all spent.

I trust in you, Lord;
I trust you'll help me, heal me, hold me,
and give me your peace. Amen.

How Great and Good You Are

The word of the Lord came to me saying,
"Before I formed you in the womb I knew you."
—Jeremiah 1:4-5

It's hard for me to wrap my mind around this, Lord,
so help my heart to understand
how you knew me before I came to be,
how you've loved me since before all time.

And while I'll never grasp the whole of it,
give me joy in simply pondering, Lord,
how great and good you are. Amen.

TO THE BEST OF MY KNOWLEDGE

To the best of my knowledge,
I'm not in charge of the universe today.

I'm only responsible for living this day
in the presence of God.

Keep me faithful, Lord,
to the work that's mine. Amen.

MOLD ME, LORD

Yet, O LORD, you are our father.
We are the clay and you the potter;
we are all the work of your hands.
—Isaiah 64:8

Like clay in your moist hands, O God,
shape me, form me, make of me
the person you desire me to be.

Turn me on the wheel of my life's
sorrows and joys
and smooth my rough places.

Touch me and let your warm fingerprints
mark me as your own.

Let me be as clay in your hands, Lord,
for you know better than I
the person you call me to be. Amen.

TEACH ME TO PRAY

Good morning, good God!

This morning, Lord,
I offer you the prayer that rolls around in my gut,
searching for words, groaning to be expressed,
not yet coming to speech.

Teach me, Lord, to know
that trusting you have heard my prayer with love
is greater than your answering my prayer
as I would have it answered.

Teach my heart to speak to your heart, Lord,
and teach my heart to hear
what your heart speaks to mine.

Teach me to trust that when I have no words to pray,
it's still a prayer to say,
"Lord, I have no words to pray."
Teach me to pray that way
and to ask for your help.

Teach me to trust that simply
to sit in your presence in silence,
without a word to say,
is to sit in your presence in prayer.

Make me mindful that I'm not alone in this, Lord;
that all who cross my path this day
wait for prayer within to come to speech,
for their hearts' silent prayers
to reach their lips.

Lord, teach me to pray
when my prayers have words
and when they don't. Amen.

You See All of Me

When I look in a mirror,
I see but a reflection, a likeness,
of who I truly am.

I'm not always happy
with what I see,
and sometimes I don't even want to look.

But when you look into my soul, Lord,
you see all of me, the whole of who I am—
and you love me nonetheless.

I don't understand this, Lord,
(how much you care for me),
and sometimes I struggle to believe it.

When you look into my heart today, Lord,
forgive, heal, mend, restore, and brighten
the broken, shaded image of your beauty
hidden deep inside me,
and help me see the person you see. Amen.

DON'T LET ME MISS YOU TODAY, LORD

You rose from the dead some two thousand years ago, Lord,
and to this day you walk among us:
your Spirit still moves in our minds and hearts.

I wonder when I'll bump into you today, Lord,
or when you'll bump into me
and turn me in the right direction.

I wonder how you'll be there for me today,
offering your peace, your strength, and your help,
and showing me how to offer it to others.

I wonder how your Spirit might enlighten my mind
with your wisdom, counsel, and truth.

I wonder how your Spirit will move in my heart,
turning me from my selfish ways
to help those in need around me.

I wonder how you'll rise in my life today, Lord:
please, don't let me miss a moment of your presence.
Amen.

Renew My Trust in You

I trust that you're with me today, Lord:
that not for a moment will you leave my side,
and at every turn you're watching my step.

I trust in your care when you answer my prayer:
"Not now . . ." or "Not yet . . ." or even just "No . . ."
Then I pray for the patience to wait and to watch
for the ways I know you'll help me get through, get by,
and survive each day's stress and the darkest of nights.

I trust that you see much more than I, Lord,
that your vision is keener than mine;
that you see all my troubles just as they are, in proportion,
the small from the large, the large from the small,
the ones I imagine from those that are real.

I trust not a word, not a thought from my prayer
will fail to echo in the depths of your heart;
that even in silence your love will abide
in the mystery and promise of your presence and peace.

So, in the quiet of my prayer, Lord,
renew and refresh my trust in you,
in your care for me.

In the silence, Lord, teach me the language
your heart speaks to mine:
a language with hardly a sound,
a language with nary a word,
the language of love that speaks so well,
much more than words might say. Amen.

How Good It Is, How Pleasant

How good it is, how pleasant,
when people dwell as one.
—Psalm 133:1

Among the people I'll meet today,
whose company I'll keep,
whether family, friend, or stranger:
help me bring peace, Lord.

May my share in others' lives
be good and pleasant;
may I dwell in peace
with all whose paths cross mine. Amen.

YOUR PLANS, NOT MINE

I know the things I really want today,
but you, Lord, know the things I truly need.

And you know how you plan
to help me find whatever I might need this day
to live in peace with you, with those around me,
and with myself.

Help me discern between my needs and wants:
make me unselfish and self-giving,
thinking first of others' needs
before my own.

And when you offer me your help,
your grace, your strength, and deeper faith:
open up my heart and hands
to take in all your gifts
with thanks and praise. Amen.

GET ME BACK ON TRACK

When I get in the way of others' peace and progress,
sit me down right away, Lord,
and give me a timeout.

When I get in my own way and litter my path
with gripes and grudges and stubborn self-pity,
then open my eyes to what's good in my life.

When I get in *your* way, Lord, and fail to follow
where I know you lead me,
reroute my GPS and get me back on track. Amen.

WHERE I AM TODAY

Help me know where I am *today*, Lord.

Help me let go of yesterday's worries
and not take on tomorrow's fears.

This is the day you've made, Lord;
it's in this moment that you're by my side.

Help me know where I am *today*, Lord.

In your eyes, Lord,
this day is filled with opportunities
for me to love and serve others
and to spend time with you in prayer.

Open my eyes and heart
to what you see, Lord,
and fill my day with your peace. Amen.

A Moment's Grace

Sometimes, Lord,
in spite of all that's going on around me,
and everything that's happening inside me,
there comes a moment's grace,
pure gift from you.

There comes a time when, without a doubt,
I know your presence in my loneliness,
your truth in my confusion,
your wisdom in my folly.

A time when I trust, deeply,
all your strength around my weakness,
your promise in my hopelessness,
your Spirit, guiding me along my way.

A time when your light fills my darkness,
your hand lifts my heavy heart,
and your mercy gently wipes my tears away.

Unexpected gifts from you:
these moments come more often than I know,
for my fear and hurt and anger blind me
and I often miss your coming near,
your strong arm reaching out to lift me up
from all that keeps me down and holds me back.

Let no graced moment pass me by,
no gift from you go missing or unopened,
no glance of healing peace escape my notice.

Today, Lord,
in spite of all that's going on around me,
and everything that's happening inside me,
send a moment of your grace, pure gift from you,
to help me know that you are with me through it all.
Amen.

Your Artistry's a Gift to Me

Was it in the dead of night, Lord,
or just before dawn?

Did you walk down my street
and climb a few trees
or reach down from heaven,
your brush in hand?

Is rusty orange your favorite hue
or just the first on this year's palette?
Will you soon return to add more color,
or wait awhile to see if I keep vigil
for the secret ways you paint the trees
while I'm asleep?

Your artistry's a gift to me and all
whose eyes are open for the hints you leave
in branches touched by gentle brushes
with divinity and grace.

In the dead of night or just before dawn,
reach down, Lord, brush in hand,
to touch my soul and leave upon it
traces of your visit and your peace. Amen.

BE THE SUN BEHIND MY CLOUDS

Like the weather, Lord, my spirits can swing
from storm to sunshine,
from sunshine to storm,
all in a day.

Be the sun behind my clouds, Lord,
and in the rain and snow,
brace and refresh me with your love today. Amen.

Let Me Overflow with Your Love

Good morning, good God!

I offer you this morning, Lord,
the moments when your Spirit opens me
to your life around me, within me,
above, before, behind, and below me.

I know there's not a moment of any day or night
when you're not by my side, Lord:
you're always there, without fail.

But I often fail to see, to hear, to sense you,
to feel your touch upon my shoulder gently guiding
or purposefully pushing me to reclaim the path
you've marked out for my steps.

I offer my desire to be open,
to recognize, to know the moments of grace
that come my way every day, every night.

I offer you my need to trust that you are with me,
especially when I fear you've left me.

I offer you my hope to find you in some special way
every day of my life,

to discover your presence and your peace
settling in around me and within me
in ways that only you would know I need.

I offer you my hunger
for the warmth of your embrace,
the light of your wisdom,
the peace of your Spirit.

And I offer you my prayer that in some way
my life will be a moment of grace
for all whose lives and paths meet mine this day.

I offer you my heart, Lord,
a cup yearning to be filled to overflowing
with the gifts you have in store for me
this morning and in the week ahead. Amen.

Bless Them with Peace

Lord, you love your people
with understanding and compassion.

With these very same gifts,
help me meet all those whose paths cross mine today,
especially those who bother and annoy me,
who don't make my day easy.

Today I'll pray especially for these folks, by name,
not asking you to change *them*, Lord,
but to bless them with your peace.

And I pray you'll change *my* heart, Lord,
with gifts of understanding and compassion. Amen.

Lord, Help My Unbelief

I'm a believer, Lord:
I have faith in you
and I trust in you.

But now and then
I wouldn't mind if you'd let me know for sure
that my belief is sound,
that my faith is not in vain,
that my trust will be rewarded.

I believe, Lord: help my unbelief.
I have faith, Lord: strengthen my confidence and conviction.
I trust you, Lord: deepen my reliance on your grace. Amen.

Branded with Your Love

I will place my law within them,
and write it upon their hearts;
I will be their God,
and they shall be my people.
—Jeremiah 31:33

I'm branded with your word, your love,
and so your word of love becomes:
the law by which I'm called to live;
the decree by which I make decisions;
the statute guiding all my choices;
the rule by which I measure what is good
and what is not.

And yet,
and yet, Lord, I often fail to live by just that word,
that love, that law so intimately written by your hand,
so personally inscribed for me to read and learn,
to know and follow.

My own desires draw my eyes from reading carefully
what you've written to instruct me,
to teach me where your way leads,
to show me how to walk in faith with you
and in peace with those whose paths I share.

In good times and in bad, Lord,
I pray you'll be my God, I pray I'll be your own:
your child, your image, your work of art divine.

So I pray that today you might refresh in me the vision of
your word, your love, your law inscribed upon my heart;
your signature, your name, your claim upon my soul;
your wisdom etched in my mind's thoughts to guide
how I decide and choose, how I discern and measure
what is good and what is not.

In the quiet of my prayer today, Lord,
write again, afresh, your word of love, your law,
upon my heart and in my mind. Amen.

Before I Open My Eyes This Morning

The folks in this house may still be sound asleep
as the sun calls them to rise,
to shine with the light that all at once
pierces their curtained windows
and reflects their Creator's glory.

Before I opened my eyes this morning, Lord,
your light was already shining on me,
the warmth of your presence calling me
to rise to the summons of a brand new day.

Cloudy or clear, snowy, raining or dry,
your light was piercing my curtained soul
and reflecting, in spite of me,
the glory that's yours to share.

In spite of me and all my fears,
in spite of my self-pity,
in spite of any burdens I bear,
let your light shine warm
in the depths of who I am.
Melt what keeps me from absorbing,
from reflecting brightly,

the brilliance of who-you-are in who-I-am
in the brand new day that summons me
to rise and shine and live,
grateful for your love. Amen.

I Don't Want to Miss a Word

No day passes until you speak to me, Lord:
in prayer, in silence, in nature,
in the words of those around me.

I wonder what you'll say to me today.

And will I be listening?

Will I hear you?

Slow me down, Lord,
and open my ears, my eyes, and my heart.

I don't want to miss a word. Amen.

THE HOLY GROUND OF YOUR PRESENCE

God said to Moses,
"Remove the sandals from your feet,
for the place where you stand is holy ground."
—Exodus 3:5

In my own little corner of the world, Lord,
show me the holy ground of your presence
in prayer, in the lives of those around me,
and even in myself.

And teach me, Lord, to take off my shoes
and walk with gentle care in your presence
and through the lives and hearts
of those whose paths cross mine. Amen.

Practicing the Golden Rule

Here's the "golden rule" that Jesus taught us:
Do to others whatever you would have them do to you.

It might help to play out that rule
and reflect and pray over its implications:

Speak to others as you'd have them speak to you.
Think of others as you'd have them think of you.
Encourage others as you'd have them encourage you.
Say of others what you'd have them say of you.
Respect others as you'd have them respect you.
Forgive others as you'd have them forgive you.

Be kind to others as you'd have them be kind to you.
Seek to understand others
as you'd have them seek to understand you.
Be honest with others
as you'd have them be honest with you.
Reach out to others
as you'd have them reach out to you.
Be just in your dealings with others
as you'd have them be just with you.

Be generous in helping others
as you'd have them be generous in helping you.
Trust others as you'd have them trust you.
Make time for others
as you'd have them make time for you.
Rejoice in others' happiness
as you'd have them rejoice in yours.
Listen to others as you'd have them listen to you.

Hang in there with others
as you'd have them hang in there with you.
Be patient with others
as you'd have them be patient with you.
Stand up for others
as you'd have them stand up for you.
Pray for others as you'd have them pray for you.
Amen.

SURRENDERING TO YOUR LOVE

Lord Jesus:
you are here now,
always
and only
because you want me
and want to be with me.

Lord Jesus:
I am here now,
again,
and only
because I want you
and want to be with you.

Lord Jesus,
help me surrender
to your love,
your mercy,
and your Holy Spirit. Amen.

Remind Me

Dear God,

When I cannot see you,
remind me that you never lose sight of me.
When I cannot hear you,
remind me that you never miss a word I pray.
When I cannot reach you,
remind me that you hold me in your arms.
When I cannot find you,
remind me that you always seek me.
When I cannot trust you,
remind me that you never give up on me.

And when I cannot, well, whatever:
remind me that you can, you do, and you will. Amen.

You Are with Me

When I see the heavens, the work of your hands,
the moon and the stars which you arranged—
who am I that you should keep me in mind,
who am I that you care for me?
—Psalm 8:4-5

I believe, Lord, that your loving eye is upon me
every moment of every day—
morning, noon, and night—
and that you never blink, never nap or nod,
but without fail you hold me in your sight.

I believe, Lord, that your ears are open to my prayer,
open to every word and thought and dream of mine,
the good ones and the bad ones:
I believe that nothing crosses my mind, stirs in my heart—
not a word leaves my lips—without your knowing it.

I believe, Lord, that your heart is open to mine 24/7/365.
Not a beat of my heart goes unnoticed by yours.
Every flutter, murmur, and skip of my heart
echoes in yours and is lovingly heard.

I trust your attention to all of my needs, Lord,
even when I wonder and worry that you've taken a break
or forgotten my name or tired of all my prayers.

I trust your response to my worries and fears
even when silence is your only response.
In your silence I trust I'm not left alone,
that I'm held in the mystery of love
waiting with me till your word, your wisdom,
your breath whispers softly,
"I am with you." Amen.

Show Up in My Life Today

O good God, good morning!

Okay—I'm going to try this again.
Look, I want to get to know you better.
I want to know you're there.
No, not *there*—
I want to know you're *here*!
And I want to know that you know me
and care about me.

Show up in my life today, Lord!
Get in my car and ride to work with me.
Be quiet, be talkative—just be there
and let me know you're there.

When we get to my job,
come in and spend the day with me.
Have a cup of coffee with me.
Take a break with me.
Sit with me at lunch: join me!

Shout in my face or whisper:
just say something and let me hear it.
Speak to me:
a sentence, a phrase, a word, a grunt.
Just break the awful silence
and say something—to me.

Unplug the ears of my heart:
break through my doubt,
my stubbornness, my pride,
and let some sound of your presence
echo within me,
anywhere inside me.

Speak, Lord.
and help me hear and trust
what you say to me;
and help me trust that you hear
what I say to you. Amen.

Praise the Lord Today!

Praise the LORD, O my soul!
I will praise the LORD all my life,
I will sing praise to my God while I live!
—Psalm 146:1-2

For what am I grateful today?
Who are the people in my life
for whom I thank my God?

Let me remember them by name
and lift them up to the Lord with a thankful heart . . .

Praise God from whom all blessings flow!
Even if this is a difficult day,
I'll remember in my prayer some better days,
and the gifts, blessings, and people who have come my way
from the heart and hand of the Lord.

I will praise my God today,
my God from whom all good gifts come.
Be still and know that God is near.
Praise the Lord today! Amen.

You Never Fail Me, Lord

What a shame, Lord, if my burdens and fears
keep me from the simple joys and blessings
you'll offer me today.

Help me see that in the hardest of times,
you don't hold back, but rather
you multiply the ways you care for me.

Let nothing keep me from seeing and hearing,
tasting and touching, knowing and enjoying
the gifts you spread along my path.

Though this day may have its troubles, Lord,
let nothing keep me from the peace and refreshment,
the grace and delights,
that come my way from your hand without fail.
Amen.

Don't Sweat the Small Stuff

Good morning, good God!

You know, Lord,
sometimes it's just the little things
that really get to me.
So this morning I offer you some of the "little things"
and pray for your healing and your help.

I offer you the little disappointments
that can sidetrack my day and distract me
from much larger concerns,
more important responsibilities.
Heal my perspective, Lord:
don't let me sweat the small stuff.
Help me to grow up
when I act like a child because things didn't go my way,
because I didn't get my way.

Heal my tunnel vision, Lord,
and my self-centered view:
let me see the big picture of my life
and of the lives of those around me.

When I'm troubled by the small things,
give me wisdom to know what truly matters,
counsel to weigh my problems wisely,
knowledge to deal with them as a believer would,
and courage to do what I must do.

Don't let the "little things" get to me, Lord.
Don't let the small stuff get between you and me
or between me and my brothers and sisters. Amen.

REFRESH ME, LORD

Good morning, good God!

Must be the time of year, Lord.
Too much going on,
too many things happening,
too many demands on everyone's energy and time,
just too much.

And though I'd like you to take it all away, Lord—
I know that's not how you work!

So I offer you my tired confusion,
my loneliness in crowds,
and feet that fail me
when I want to run from it all.

When too many things are happening all at once,
help me see what's important and what's not;
help me know what you'd have me do first, Lord—
and what you'd not have me do at all.

Give me wisdom to know what you ask of me, Lord,
and strength to accomplish what's mine to do.
Speak to my heart and with your word,
open my heart to your will.

I pray for your strength and counsel:
when my heart's slow to know where to turn,
where to go, what to do,
encourage and lead and guide me.

Rouse me when I'm tired, Lord.
Give me your strength when mine fails and
help me spend it on what's good and fruitful
for me, for others,
for all whose paths cross mine.

Lift me up when I'm bowed down, Lord.
Refresh your spirit within me;
renew my hope and trust in you;
give me a new beginning this day. Amen.

Every Good Gift Comes from You

Without a single exception, Lord,
every good gift in my life
comes from you.

The family and friends who love and care for me,
who listen to me and accept me,
who guide me and challenge and comfort me:
every one of them is your gift to me.

Every step I take in the right direction,
every decision I make that's honest and fair,
every change I make to be true to myself,
every thought I have that leads to peace,
every deed I do to help another:
every one of these is a gift of your prompting.

Every time I stop to look within,
every moment I pause to ask your pardon,
every prayer I whisper to ask for help,
every time I thank you for all my gifts,
every thought I have that leads to you:
every one of these is your gift to me,
your Spirit moving deep within me.

Without a single exception, Lord,
every good gift in my life
comes from you.

For all of these I praise and thank you, Lord.
Amen.

GIVE ME THE GRACE I'LL NEED, LORD

Love is patient, love is kind.
—1 Corinthians 13:4

Lord, it's likely that sometime today
someone will try my patience,
someone will test my kindness.

Give me the grace I'll need
to respond with the patience and kindness
you always offer me. Amen.

Loving Those around Me

Lord, my heart hungers for love:
I want to love you,
and I want to know your love for me.

But I cannot love you
and I cannot know your love for me
apart from loving my neighbor.

So, today, Lord,
help me love my neighbor,
especially the one I have trouble loving,
so that in loving those around me,
I might grow in love of you,
and come to know your love for me. Amen.

Every Day Is a New Canvas

Sometimes, Lord,
my life seems just the "same old-same old,"
day in, day out,
over and over again.

I easily get caught in this cycle,
going nowhere fast, losing sight of hope
and all that tomorrow might hold.

But every day's a new canvas, Lord,
if I pick up my paints and my brushes.

Every day's a blank sheet of paper
waiting for me to write a new chapter.

Every day's a fresh lump of clay
waiting for me to mold and shape and sculpt.

Every day has twenty-four hours
waiting to show what you'd have me see,
to speak what you'd have me hear,
to lead where you'd have me go,
to open my heart to something new,
to the promise of what's yet to be.

Shake me free of the same-old, same-old,
and waken me, Lord, to the day at hand,
the day you offer, the day you've made
for me to live anew. Amen.

Help Me Return to You

My sacrifice, O God, is a contrite spirit;
a heart contrite and humbled, O God,
you will not spurn.
—Psalm 51:17

The truth is, Lord,
I have sins I'm not sure I'm sorry for.

I know I've done things against your law,
outside the bounds of your love,
things I'm not proud of:
things I thought I needed to do,
things I wanted to do,
things I thought I had to do—
and so I did them . . .

I've sinned in ways I thought I never would, Lord,
and now it's hard to name those things
I thought I'd never do.

Help me return to you, Lord,
with my heart's burden of sins so hard to name.

My pride keeps me from facing what I've done,
and my fear keeps me from naming how I've failed,
but your grace helps me pray for pardon.

Help me face the bad decisions I've made,
the choices I wish I hadn't had to face,
the wounds my soul must bare for you to heal
that I might come home to you with all my heart.

Give me a spirit of repentance, Lord.
Help me name my sins and know your mercy:
a heart contrite and humbled
you'll never turn away.

I trust your mercy, Lord,
and pray you'll bring me back to you
with all my heart. Amen.

Open My Heart

In the next twenty-four hours, Lord,
open my eyes and ears
to all you want me
to see and hear.

Open my mind
to what you'd have me ponder
and open my heart to all
you call me to love.

Open my hands to help anyone
in need of my strength,
my comfort, my compassion.

Open my mouth to speak
only the words
that others need to hear.

Open my day to find the time
to sit with you alone,
to open up my heart to you.

And especially, Lord,
when I want to give in,
when I want to shut down:
open me up, refresh my spirit,
and help me begin again,
and again,
and again. Amen.

Today Is a Gift

Good morning, good God!

I want to offer you gifts from who I am, Lord,
today, this morning, this week.

I want to offer you what I have right now.
Not what I've lost and wish I still had.
Not what I hope to find but haven't yet.

I want to offer you the heart of me,
who I am, today.

What I have this day is unfinished, Lord.
It's incomplete, has rough edges,
isn't as pretty nor near as neat as I wish it were.
But it's what I have.

As I lift it up to you,
I see that it's falling apart in a few places.
And the patches on old mistakes are showing
just in the places I wish they didn't show.

Help me see the beauty you see in what I offer.
Help me look beyond its unfinished edges.
Help me to accept what's falling apart
as work for your mending hand.
Help me learn to love the patches
as the places where you've healed me.
Help me see that it's the giver, not the gift, you love
and that my simple gifts are but the tokens
that bring us close together.

Accept me, Lord, as I am,
and receive what I have to offer.

And most of all,
open me to the gift of this day,
the day you've given me. Amen.

Help Me to Know Your Nearness

In the morning let me know your love / for I put my trust in you.
Make me know the way I should walk: / to you I lift up my soul . . .
Let your good spirit guide me / in ways that are level and smooth.
—Psalm 143:8, 10

Sometimes, Lord, I don't know which way to turn,
which path to take, what to do next,
or what you ask of me today.

Open my heart this morning to your good Spirit,
to counsel and guide me,
to show me the path you'd have me walk.
Help me to trust you'll be at my side
from the time I get out of bed in the morning
until I fall asleep tonight.

Show me the path leveled by your wisdom, Lord:
show me the smooth road where I won't stumble or fall.

And along the way,
help me to rest in the stillness of your presence
and to know, Lord, that you are near today. Amen.

Get In My Face Today, Lord!

Get in my face today, Lord:
walk right up to me and look me in the eye!

Be obvious—not subtle.
Speak up—don't whisper.
Block my path—don't let me miss you.

Grab my shoulder, turn me around,
and point me where you know I need to go.

Make a difference in my day, Lord,
and help me make a difference
in the lives of those around me. Amen.

TRUST FOR TODAY

Lord,
there's not a soul you don't love,
there's not a prayer you don't hear,
there's no anger you can't tame,
there's no sin you won't forgive,
there's not a heart you won't heal,
there's not a tear you fail to notice,
there's no pain you haven't felt,
there's no fear you can't relieve,
there's not a mind you cannot read,
there's not a worry you can't ease,
there's not a joy you don't share,
there's not a problem you can't solve,
there's no trouble I face without your help.

When I need to remember one or two of these,
or more, or all of the above,
bring me back to this prayer, Lord,
and to my trust in you today. Amen.

THE WIND OF YOUR SPIRIT

Good morning, good God!

The wind of your Spirit
fills the sheets of my soul,
gently guiding me in seas I've never sailed
for fear of shoals I have not known—
while your grace charts my course
steering me to parts and people new—
and with a purpose all your own.

Poke, push, prompt, and prod me, Lord,
to waken to your word, calling me
to life more joyful, free, and faithful
than all my days thus far.

Open my eyes and ears to those
whose paths cross mine,
who may not yet have felt the gentle press
your grace now places on their hearts.

Good God of morning
and of every starry night,
I praise you for the gift and grace
of every day this week. Amen.

Bend My Heart to Your Will

Bend my heart to do your will
and not to love of gain.
Keep my eyes from what is false:
by your word, give me life.
—Psalm 119:36-37

Bend my heart today, Lord,
to see you more clearly,
love you more dearly,
follow you more nearly.
Bend my heart to know you,
to understand—and to do—what you ask of me.

Keep my gaze from what's false,
from whatever leads me off the path of your truth.
Open me to your word, Lord,
to the counsel I need,
to the wisdom that's only yours to give.

Bend my heart to your will
and open my eyes to the light of your presence.
Bend my heart to the stillness, Lord,
and help me know that you are my God,
that you are near. Amen.

Make Me Your Holy Temple

Good morning, good God!

You choose me
to be a temple of your presence,
to be a home for your Spirit,
to hold something holy within me.

You trust me to hold you
in my heart, in my mind,
in my hands, in my soul,
in my imagination, in my body.

You trust me to hold you within me,
to hold your Spirit within me
even as you hold me.

It's easy for me to say,
"I'm not worthy to be your temple."
It's harder for me to say,
"I want to be worthy."

But this morning, Lord,
that's my prayer. Amen.

My Simple Prayer

I make prayer a complicated affair, Lord,
when I worry about what to say,
and *how* to say it and the *right* way to say it—
as if you might possibly turn down my prayer
because I stumbled in finding the "right words,"
or found no words at all
to speak all my heart might hold.

I don't need special words, Lord,
and I know you're pleased
when I "make it up as I go along"
with words that come not from a book
but from my heart.

I forget that it's you who calls me to prayer, Lord,
that you know what's on my mind and in my heart
even before I think to pray.

I offer you my uncomplicated prayer, Lord,
and ask you to receive me
into the simplicity of your presence and your heart.

Remind me, Lord, that in my spiritual life the rule is,
"The simpler the better!"
You love all simple things, Lord:
show me how you love my simple self
and love my simple prayer.

Receive my simple morning prayer, Lord:
I offer it today and all through the week ahead. Amen.

Another Day to Live for Jesus!

O, good God, good morning!

You've given me another day to live, Lord:
a day to shape into something beautiful,
a day to serve others, a day to give you thanks,
a day in the life of you and me, Lord.

How would you have me spend my day, Lord?
With whom would you have me share it?
Along what path will your Spirit draw me?
Close to whose heart will your heart lead me?

What word would you have me speak this day?
What quiet time together have you planned for us?
What tears might I cry today, Lord?
And with what joy will you touch my soul?

When I'm tired today, Lord, give me strength.
When I'm moving too fast, slow me down.
When I'm saying too much, let me know.
When I need to speak, give me words to say.

Give me patience with this day's routine, Lord,
and open my eyes to see what's fresh and new.
Because this day comes from your hand, it is blessed,
and when I offer it back to you, it is a gift.

O, good God, good morning!
Keep me safe until I say good night. Amen.

I Ask for Your Spirit, Lord

I have some important tasks ahead of me, Lord,
and some of them won't be easy to accomplish:
the kind of work that makes me worry a lot
and leads me to doubt myself.

So I ask you to help me do the right things
and to do them well.

I ask for courage to speak the truth
and to speak it with charity and conviction.

I ask for your wisdom to help me discern
and know what you ask and expect of me.

I ask for your mercy to lift me up if I fail
and to set me on your path again.

I ask for your strength lest I grow weary:
keep me equal to the tasks at hand.

I ask for your Spirit, Lord, to guard me
and guide me in all things, in your peace. Amen.

LIVING FOR YOU TODAY

The fool says in his heart,
"There is no God above.". . .
God looks down from heaven . . .
to see if any are wise,
if any seek God.
—Psalm 53:1, 2

When you look for the wise, Lord,
you look not just for those who say they believe in you,
but for those who live according to what they believe.

Help me, a believer, live what I believe, Lord.
Let me take some time today to renew my belief in you
and to ask you to help me live as I believe.
Give me a time and place to be quiet today
and help me pray.

In the stillness and in the peace,
let me know that you are near,
because I believe that you are God above
and I believe you are God beside me. Amen.

Make Us Grateful, Lord

Dear God,

Our lives are your gift to us,
as fragile as they are strong.
From day to day, with all our care and vigilance,
we still don't know what might befall us.

We pray for those around the world
whose daily lives are much more tenuous than our own—
especially for the poor and the homeless.

We pray you'll send your Holy Spirit
to draw us, the strong and stable in the global village,
to offer and use everything at our disposal
to reach out and serve those in need, in dire need,
in daily, dire need.

We thank you for the prosperity and safety that are ours,
and ask you to never let us take these for granted.
Give us generous hearts:
we have so much more than we need.
Help us to remember that all good gifts come from you
and are "on loan" to us to share with others.

Make us as watchful for the needs of those far away
as we are for those who live under our own roofs,
in our parish and town and in our nation.

Make us grateful for all we have,
especially for families, friends, and faith.
May our thanksgiving never cease to flow from our hearts.
May our praise become the deeds of caring for others.

We pray in the name of Jesus,
who is Lord for ever and ever. Amen.

I Offer All Hearts to You

Good morning, good God!

As this day breaks, O loving Lord,
I offer you the joys of all
who will today find help, a friend, a love, a cure,
some work, some rest, some food, some time to laugh.

I offer you the heavy hearts
of those bent low by sorrow and grief, by loss and tears,
the hearts of all who cry and call your name.

I offer you the joys of those
who will this day find healing, hope, and trust in you,
a deeper faith, forgiveness, truth, and peace.

I offer you the wounded hearts
of those who've lost so much—too much—in love, in war,
in promises long broken, never kept.

I offer you the faith of hearts
that reach out for your hand
when strength for reaching's gone,
when hunger for your touch is all there is.

I offer you the hope of hearts
who seek your peace when peace is nowhere to be found,
who seek your face when darkness clouds the sun.

I offer you the love of hearts,
remembering better days and trusting you
will come again and keep your word of promised peace.

I offer you all hearts, O Lord:
our joyful, sorrowed souls are yours both night and day;
receive and bless and heal them with your grace. Amen.

THE GIFT OF PEOPLE

For the gift of people who listen to me,
for the grace of folks who forgive me,
for the wisdom of those who correct me,
for the favor of friends who endure me,
for the strength of those who support me,
for the care of all who love me,
thank you, Lord!

Help *me*, Lord,
to listen, forgive, correct, abide,
support, and care for others
as patiently and faithfully as I'm so generously loved.

Open my eyes and ears and heart, Lord,
to someone who needs my help today,
someone who needs my time,
my love and understanding.

As you are there for me, Lord,
let me be there for all today. Amen.

No One Loves Me like You

Lord,
No one knows me
as well as you do.
No one understands me
the way you do.
No one's as patient with me
as you are.
No one watches over me
as carefully as you do.
No one's more faithful to me
than you are.
No one judges me
more mercifully than you do.
No one forgives me
as freely, as fully as you do.

So for all your gifts and grace,
for your mercy and your love,
I thank you, Lord,
for I have no God but you.

Only you, Lord,
only you. Amen.

GIVE ME HOPE, LORD

Lord, I am so easily weighed down
by my struggles, my burdens,
by the harsh reality of my daily life.

Sometimes I think I'll lose hope
in you, in tomorrow, in myself,
and I need you to help me see
that the peace I imagine,
the peace I pray for,
the peace you promise
is greater than any of my problems.

Help me trust that my future, Lord,
is not limited by my present trials,
that the troubles of the moment
will not have the last word,
that my burdens are prelude to joy.

Give me hope in my suffering
for that is the path of your love,
and let my hope never forget
the suffering of which it was born.

Show me how the troubles of today
prepare me for the advent of your peace
and the gift of your grace.

Come, Lord Jesus, be with me
and be my hope! Amen.

WHISPERED WORDS OF GRACE

Slow me down today, Lord,
and whisper a word or two
in the quiet of my mind and heart.

When I'm cursing myself or others,
whisper words of blessing.
When I'm judging others' words and deeds,
whisper words of mercy.
When I've failed and when I've sinned,
whisper words of pardon.
When I'm facing loss and grief,
whisper words of consolation.
When I'm stuck in my own foolishness,
whisper words of wisdom.
When I'm confounded and confused,
whisper words of counsel.
When I'm caught up in my lies,
whisper words of truth.
When life is just too tough to take,
whisper words of hope.

When my heart is wounded, hurt, and broken,
whisper words of healing.
When I'm at war within myself or with my neighbor,
whisper words of peace.
When my voice is still and silent,
whisper words of prayer for me to speak.

But first of all, Lord, slow me down
and help me find a quiet place
where I can hear your whispered words of grace.
Amen.

What If, Lord?

Good morning, good God!

This morning, Lord,
I'm wondering:
What if?

What if I accepted all the love you offer me?
How would I change and grow?
How would my relationships change and grow?
How would I be a different person?

What if I stopped to listen
and really tried to hear what you ask of me?
What would I hear?
What would I do differently?
What new turns might my life take?

What if I saw you in every face I meet?
Especially in the faces where I cannot find you now?
How would my day change? My plans?
With whom would I be spending my time?

What if I named and counted my sins
and prayed and asked for your mercy?

How would my heart be changed?
How might I become more forgiving of others?

What if I put others' needs
ahead of my own for a whole week?
How would my priorities readjust?
What would I need to let go of?
How would such a week be different than last week?

What if I walked only the path you map out for me?
Where would you lead me? Where would I go?
How would my direction change?
Who and what would I leave behind?

What if I trusted you, Lord?
What if I trusted your love for me?
What if I trusted your plan for me?
What if I trusted that I am yours
and that you will never abandon me,
that you will always be with me,
and that by your side I have nothing to fear?

What if, Lord; what if? Amen.

The Holy Oil of Grace

Lord, put a sticker on the windshield of my soul
to remind me when my prayer life needs a tune-up—
and I'm thinking I might need one pretty soon.

My filter needs a thorough cleaning,
screening out what's clogging up
what fuels the engine of my being.

My prayer life won't turn over; it misfires,
and your Spirit's charged ignition
is the spark I need to start me up again.

Lord, filter all the air I breathe
and keep from my heart's valves
whatever keeps me far from you.

My soul's old timing belt is worn and fails
to sync my needs and fears with time to pray
for you to manage my combustion.

I need a fluid faith for power steering through hard times,
for braking when I need to stop and think—
and stop and think again.

I need the holy oil of grace
to keep me running smooth and clean
in thought, in word, in deed.

Lord, put a sticker on the windshield of my soul
to remind me when my prayer life needs a tune-up—
and I'm thinking I might need one pretty soon. Amen.

LET ME PRAISE YOU EVERY DAY!

I will bless the Lord at all times,
his praise shall be ever in my mouth.
—Psalm 34:1

It's easy to praise you on the good days, Lord,
when all's well and the road is smooth.

But give me faith and strength
to praise you *every* day,
especially when the skies are gray
and the road uneven.

May my heart bless you at *all* times, Lord,
and your praise be *always* on my lips. Amen.

Loving My Neighbor

Help me, Lord:
to do no wrong to my neighbor today,
to do no wrong to my family,
to do no wrong to my friends,
to do no wrong to my enemies,
to do no wrong to my co-workers,
to do no wrong to strangers,
to do no wrong to myself.

Help me, Lord,
to love you today
before and above all others,
and to love my neighbor as myself. Amen.

A Prayer of Gratitude

Good morning, good God!

I come to you grateful for all
the good and holy folks whose paths
cross mine and help me find my way.

I come with thanks for all the ways
so many share their lives with me
and bless me every day.

I give you thanks for helping hands,
strong shoulders, open minds,
and hearts in tune with yours.

I thank you for the peace that's mine
from others, shared, with plenty left
for those who need what I have found.

I thank you for the patient ones
who give and bide their time with me
and slow my harried, hurried steps.

And thanks for those who help me place,
with wisdom far beyond my ken,
the puzzled pieces of my life.

I praise you for the gracious ways
you draw us into one another's lives
and bind our needs and gifts as one.

As I am blessed by others' gifts,
let my gifts, too, a blessing be
in thanks for all that I've received.

This prayer I offer gratefully
this morning, Lord, this day, this night,
and through the week ahead. Amen.

Help Me Pay Attention, Lord

Among all the distractions
whirling within and around me,
help me stop each day to pause, to pray,
to pay attention to you, Lord.

Help me pay attention
to how you pay attention to me:
24/7, ever watchful in your vigil,
day and night.

Help me attend to the words you speak,
whispered in my heart,
words to guard and guide me
and keep me from harm's way.

Help me attend to your Spirit
moving in my thoughts and plans;
help me attend to what you ask of me
and walk the path you chart for me today.

Help me pay attention to all whose paths
will intersect with mine today.

Help me attend to their burdens and their needs
and what gifts of peace they offer me.

Make me mindful, Lord, of you:
help me pause for prayer and in the quiet just sit still,
attending to the silence of your presence. Amen.

Help Me Do unto Others

Bless your persecutors, bless and do not curse them.
Rejoice with those who rejoice, weep with those who weep.
Have the same attitude toward all.
—Romans 12:14-16

How grateful I am, Lord,
that *you* have the same attitude toward everyone
—including me!

You love the sinner as you love the saint.
You love the faithful and the unfaithful alike.
You welcome the prayers of stumblers and mumblers
as you welcome the chants of holy monks.
You love the efforts of those who fail
as much as the deeds of those who succeed.
You're as close to me wherever I wander
as you are to those who never stray.
You have the same attitude toward all, Lord,
and nothing about me keeps you from loving me.

But don't let me presume on your love, Lord;
don't let me take it for granted.
Call me to be more faithful;
walk me away from my sins.

Help me know what you ask of me
and give me the courage to do it.
Help me, Lord, to love those who don't love me;
help me to love and not reject them.
Open my heart to share in others' joys
and to stand by them in their grief.
Help me do unto others, Lord,
as I'd have them do unto me. Amen.

WAIT WITH ME, LORD

I'm sure to spend a good part of this day waiting.

I'll wait for people to arrive and leave,
I'll wait for things to happen—or not,
I'll wait for time to pass and a new day to come.

I'll wait for meetings to begin and be over,
I'll wait for calls, for mail, and for answers to questions,
I'll wait for breaks for coffee and for lunch.

And I'll wait for you, Lord:
I'll wait for you to show your face and speak a word
of comfort or of challenge—perhaps a word of mercy.

I'll wait for myself, too, when I stall,
when I'm behind and holding back
in so many different ways.

Yes, I'm sure to spend a good part of this day waiting.

Wait with me, Lord:
be patient and wait with me—
it's so hard to wait alone. Amen.

An Amazing Grace

I try to make time for prayer—
as though there might be anything in life
more important than spending time with you.
I forget that unlike busy old me,
you're always ready to meet me in prayer,
never too busy to sit down with me
or take a walk by my side.
Your calendar is always open for me;
you're never too busy to get together for a while
or just to meet, quietly, in the world behind my eyes,
closed for just a moment.

What an amazing grace, Lord!
I finally make time to pray,
I'm not even sure what to say—
and you're simply pleased
that I've come to you. Amen.

ACCEPTING THE DAY AS IT COMES

Lord,
You know everything that's going to happen
in my life today.

Lacking that knowledge,
I might worry and fret over what I don't know,
second guessing all I say and do,
hiding from things I need not fear.

What a waste of a day, Lord!

So I pray for the faith and trust I need
to accept this day as it comes,
to place my day in your hands,
and to live this day in your peace. Amen.

THE CRIES OF THE POOR

The Lord hears the cry of the poor;
blessed be the Lord!
—From the song based on Psalm 34

Open my heart, Lord, to hear the cry of the poor
and to respond generously
where I can supply what others need.

Open my ears to hear the cry
of those right around me
and to respond as gently and graciously
as I am able.

As you hear the cry of the poor,
and of all your people,
let me hear them, too, Lord, today. Amen.

LORD, GIVE ME PERSPECTIVE

Lord, I'm so easily consumed
by my own worries and problems,
looming larger than life in my fears and my dreams.

I need some perspective, a wider angle,
a longer view for seeing what's real,
what's great, and what's small.

Lord, give me perspective through praying for others.
Let me pray for the dying and the critically ill,
for all those in prison or unjustly bound.
Let me pray for the homeless, the poor on the streets,
those without medicine, water, and food.

Let me pray for the lonely, forgotten, and lost;
for innocent victims of terror and war.
Let me pray for the abandoned, the abused, and addicted,
and for all who suffer alone.

Let me pray for those who have no friends,
no one to lean on when times are tough.
Let me pray for those who have no hope, no faith,
no God to pray to when worries and problems
loom larger than life in their fears and dreams.

Give me some perspective, Lord,
a wider angle, a longer view for seeing what's real,
what's great, and what's small
in my mind and life today. Amen.

Turning Down the Volume
to Hear You

Lord,
I know you speak to me all day long
and even through the night
while I'm asleep.

You speak in my prayer,
in my heart, my mind, and my dreams,
in my hopes and fears, in my thoughts
and in my conscience.

Sometimes your voice is loud and clear,
but often it's hushed and subtle;
just a whisper,
a quiet shifting in my soul.

Sometimes I hear you plainly,
but I often miss the word you speak:
the volume of life around me
is turned so high and full
that I can hardly hear myself think,
let alone listen for you and hear
your voice and the words you speak within me.

Help me find a time and place today, Lord,
to turn down the volume,
to hush the noise around me
and listen carefully
for the word you speak to me today. Amen.

COME, HOLY SPIRIT OF GOD!

Come, Holy Spirit of God!
Refresh your vital presence in my mind, my heart,
my thoughts, and my imagination.
Open me to your gifts
and lead me to rely on them.
Give me the grace to be Spirit-driven.
Descend upon the world
and make your dwelling in the hearts of all.
Set me on fire for the reign of peace
you offer in your gifts.

Come, Holy Spirit of God!
Draw me out of myself, my comfort, my contentment,
and lead me to where God's grace awaits.
Draw me out of my inertia, my laziness, my corner,
and lead me along the path of God's desire for me.

Free me from the prison of my fears and mistrust,
and with courage, with fire, lead me by your light.
Amen. ∾

HELP ME SIMPLIFY, LORD

Help me simplify my life, Lord.
Help me give away, give up,
clean out, cast off,
do without, strip away
the many things I do not need.
Help me empty my heart
of things that cannot offer
what my heart was meant to hold.

And make me generous, Lord,
in sharing and giving away
the things I have in plenty,
for which others have so great a need.

Help me see the needs
of those whose paths cross mine today, Lord,
and open my heart to be ready to give freely,
without counting the cost. Amen.

I Take So Many Things for Granted

I take so many things for granted, Lord:
my life, my health, my work,
my family and my friends,
the freedom of my homeland,
the roof over my head and the food on my table.

Help me grow in appreciation and gratitude
for all that I have, for all that comes my way each day,
for the bounty I enjoy in a world
where so many go without.

Help me grow in generously sharing what I have
when so often I have so much more than what I need,
and sometimes even more than I want.

Help me simplify, simplify, simplify!

And most of all, Lord,
help me not take *you* for granted.

Help me not take for granted
the love you freely share.

Help me not take your patience for granted,
excusing myself for how slowly I change,
how slowly I grow in trust and faith.

Help me not take your pardon for granted:
I don't deserve or merit your mercy—
the greatest gift I could ever receive.

Help me not take your presence for granted:
you never leave my side,
no matter how often or how far
I wander from your path.

Help me not take anything about you for granted, Lord,
for there is in my life nothing greater
than the hope I find in you
and in your love for me. Amen.

Courage for Today

I offer you, Lord, this day, this week,
and every hour in it.

I offer the hours that seem days' long,
the days that seem like weeks,
and the weeks that have no end.

Help me trust that in your company
I'll come to this day's end, to Sunday's rest
and season's change,
safe and secure
in your company, in your presence,
and in your strength when mine is spent.

I offer you my memories, Lord,
of hours, days, weeks, of months and years
I thought I'd not survive but did,
and I pray that you refresh in me the courage I need
to live my life a day at a time, an hour at a time,
secure in your strong arms.

Keep me mindful, Lord,
of others who stand before this day
unsure of where it will lead and take them:
help us all be understanding and gentle with one another,
offering support where it's needed,
accepting others' help when it's offered.

I offer you this day, Lord,
as long or short as it may seem,
and trust that this day's end
will find me by your side
and you by mine. Amen. ∽

Nourishing Those around Me

Who doesn't long and pray
for restful nights and peaceful days?

Who doesn't hope and wait for an end
to days of worried fears and pray
for nights of good, deep sleep?

Has anyone a heart not aching
to be known, loved, accepted—
no strings attached?

Do I know another whose desires
are that much different from my own?

We're all much more alike than not;
in our souls, our similarities
outnumber our disparities.

From the same place deep within
we share a common thirst,
and only those who know our hunger
know the love that feeds our heart.

Help me, Lord, to see, know, and nourish
all the hearts of those around me,
and open up my heart to all
who'd love and feed and nourish me. Amen.

WHAT A BEAUTIFUL VIEW, LORD!

What a beautiful view, Lord!
It's true:
on a clear day you can see forever—
well, almost.

But in my own life,
lost in the woods
counting needles on pine trees,
I often fail to look up
to see the light on the horizon.

Just a tilt of my head
would lift my eyes
to the beauty you set before me.

Help me see as you see, Lord:
give me the long view,
and help me look beyond the troubles of the day
to see what lies ahead.

Chuck me under the chin
and draw my gaze to yours,
until I find in you the grace I need
to rise up with new purpose.

Give me courage to walk the path
through the forest of my fears,
out of the woods, to the water's edge,
where your peaceful presence
beckons me to come. Amen.

SLOW ME DOWN

Slow me down, Lord:
when I can't stop the merry-go-round on my own,
slow me down.

When my ears and mind are filled with noise,
slow me down,
and show me a path to a quiet place.

When I'm standing still
but inside moving at 60 miles per hour,
put the brakes on, Lord:
slow me down
and bring me to a stop right by your side.

Bring me to a quiet place
where I can hear my own breathing
and know the breath of your Spirit within me.

Help me savor the silence
and find some peace of mind and heart
in the quiet, in my soul.

Bring me to a quiet place *today*, Lord,
whenever, wherever that might be.

Help me make the time to sit with you
and find the peace that's only yours to give.

Slow me down today, Lord,
that I might be still, at peace,
and know that you are God.

Today, Lord,
please slow me down, today. Amen.

At Daybreak

Good morning, good God!

Wake me before the alarm clock rings
and rouse me to a new day, rain or shine;
fill me at daybreak with your kindness, Lord,
and let the sun rise in my heart.

Even in my dreams, fill me with your peace
and calm my soul before the dawn's first light;
before my eyes are open, when I'm still half asleep,
stir my mind to thoughts of how this day's your gift to me.

If clouds above or clouds within should tempt my heart
to doubt that you are with me, by my side:
shake me wide awake and pierce the mist
that veils and hides your face from mine.

At daybreak fill me with your kindness
and give my heart a day's supply of hope and trust;
let my first thoughts be of you, Lord,
my first words give you praise for this day's light.

At daybreak fill me with your Spirit's gifts
to help me face whatever comes my way,
and give me strength and faith in you
and in your promise to be with me every step along my path.

At daybreak fill me with the grit I need
to face whatever I might fear or hide from:
remind me that I'm not alone, that with you, Lord,
and by your side, I need not be afraid.

At daybreak pull me from my bed and set me on my feet:
shower me with grace until I'm wide-eyed, braced
and ready for a brand new day, a day I've never known,
the day that you have readied for my soul.

At daybreak and throughout this day and into night,
be at my side and show your face, Lord,
and let me hear your voice, calling me to listen
and to live the word you speak within my heart. Amen.

Be There for Me, Lord

O God,
Help me to know how much I need you.

And if I think I don't need you,
or that I can get by without you some days,
some months—and even years—
then open my eyes to my foolishness,
and lead me home to you.

I need you to be there for me, Lord;
I need you to come on my behalf
to be my strength, my guide,
my advocate, my help, and my Savior.

Teach me to hunger for time with you, for prayer.
Teach me to thirst for your truth,
your wisdom, and your counsel.

Teach me to long for the peace
that only you can give,
the peace I so much need.

Show me how I am poor, Lord,
show me how poor I am
and how your grace is the greatest treasure
I will ever possess.

You hear the cry of the poor, Lord:
Hear the cry of my poor heart,
and help me hear the cry of those in need. Amen.

LIFT UP MY CHIN

Good morning, good God!

I offer you my thanks, Lord,
for the gifts I so often and so easily miss
when I'm focused on myself, on my own needs,
my own disappointments.

How many times have you reached out to me,
and I've missed you, Lord,
because I would not lift my drooping chin
or open my eyes to see beyond my sadness.

Your gifts are so many, Lord.
Some come like a spring shower,
raining down on everyone in sight,
and now and again comes one
marked with my name and signed with yours,
something others might not even see,
but that I recognize as a token of your love,
a sign of your presence, a reason to believe.

Lift my chin and open my eyes, Lord,
that I might notice the gifts you send this day,
and help me find at least the ones
my heart needs most. Amen.

Two-Word Prayers

Calm me,
quiet me,
settle me . . .

Steady me,
balance me,
ground me . . .

Plant me,
root me,
embed me . . .

Support me,
sustain me,
protect me . . .

Forgive me,
pardon me,
free me . . .

Refresh me,
restore me,
heal me . . .

Enfold me,
embrace me,
hold me . . .

Lord, hear my prayer today!
Amen.

Lord, Let Me Find Rest

There are times, Lord,
when I think you run me ragged
just to wear me out and slow me down,
because you know that when I'm tired,
I'm more open to what's simple,
to what's real and true and good.

And I see how much I need your help,
how weak I am without you,
how much I need your strength.

I'm tired now, run ragged, and open to your grace:
Come simplify my life, and in your peace
let me find rest. Amen.

BY YOUR GRACE

But by the grace of God I am what I am,
and his grace to me has not been ineffective.
—1 Corinthians 15:10

I am what I am, Lord:
the beautiful work of your hands,
desirous of doing your will,
broken, in need of your mercy,
thirsty for wisdom and truth,
wanting to live by your word.

By your grace, Lord, for there is no other way,
help me find the peace of becoming
the person you made me to be. Amen.

GIVE ME SAFE HARBOR

*[Thus says the L*ORD*,]*
"If you remove from your midst oppression,
false accusation and malicious speech . . .
then light shall rise for you in the darkness."
—Isaiah 58:9, 10

No doubt about it, Lord:
my heart too often harbors ill will,
where harsh judgments dock
and angry words float freely,
riding dark waves of envy.

A harbor clouded and choked
with wrecks of grudges
and dregs drawn up from murky deeps.

A cold cove it is, craving warmth,
and a sea change of your grace:
Rescue me from this shipwreck, Lord!

Help me unload my heart's hold
of words and wishes stored only for hurt.

Sweeten the stale waters my soul sails,
and fill me with a cargo of kindness,
such as I seek from others.

Rise like the sun over my heart's bow,
and with the dawn's warmth
cleanse and heal me.

I trust you, Lord,
and I pray you'll sail me home
to the refuge of the harbor of your heart,
over waters of your grace. Amen.

THANK YOU, LORD!

Thank you, Lord,
for getting me over bumps in the road
I thought were mountains.

Thank you for guiding me through days and nights
I thought impossible, impassable.

Thank you for helping me accomplish
what I never thought I could.

Help me hold on to these memories, Lord:
I'll need their promise tomorrow.

Help me stay close by your side, Lord;
I know I can't make it alone.

With you by my side,
with your hand on my shoulder,
my troubles are halved, Lord,
and all my joys are doubled. Amen.

THE LORD IS MY LIGHT

You, O LORD, are my lamp,
my God who lightens my darkness.
With you I can break through any barrier,
with my God I can scale any wall.
—Psalm 18:28-29

When I stumble in my own darkness today,
will I trust the light of your presence, Lord,
to light my way, my path?
When I'm alone, helpless and stuck—
unable to budge, to move ahead, to gain some ground:
will I pray and rely on you, will I trust in your strength
to help me along, to see me through,
to help me scale the heights ahead?
Lord, be my light, my way, my help, and my strength
today and through the night.
Be still, my soul, and know that God is near. Amen.

GOD IS HERE

Who will separate us from the love of Christ?
Trial, or distress, or persecution, or hunger,
or nakedness, or danger, or the sword? . . .
Yet in all this we are more than conquerors
because of him who has loved us.
—Romans 8:35, 37

Show me your love, Lord—today.
Show me how your love is greater than this day's anxiety,
this day's worries, this day's sadness,
this day's trials and distress.

Show me your love, Lord—today.
Show me how your love is greater than those I fear,
those who've harmed me, those I envy,
those who haunt my dreams and memories.

Show me your love, Lord—today,
and how the love you have for me is stronger
than anything or anyone threatening to part me
from the promise of your presence by my side.

Help me remember, Lord,
that nothing is going to happen today
that you and I can't handle together—
and that when I'm weak and fearful,
your love will supply the strength I'm wanting.

In the quiet of my prayer, Lord,
help me take a deep breath and trust in you
and in the strength you have in store to help me.

In the stillness here, let me know that you are near,
that you are by my side, that with your help
there's nothing ahead I need to fear.

Stay close enough to take my hand, O Lord:
put your hand on my shoulder
and remind me that nothing can come between us,
that nothing will separate me from your abiding love.
Amen.

GIVE ME WISDOM

The Wisdom of God can do all things
and renews everything while herself enduring. . . .
Indeed, she reaches from end to end mightily
and governs all things well.
—Wisdom 7:27; 8:1

Do I dare ask for Wisdom, Lord?
Do I truly want to be wise in thought, in word, in deed?

Wisdom comes at no small cost:
To welcome her into my heart
is to bid goodbye to my soul's foolish adolescence,
my selfish pride, my reliance on myself for truth.
A demanding and jealous lover Wisdom is:
she will countenance no other claims upon my heart,
but will ask for all I have to give
in return for more than I might hope or dream.

She will seduce me with the truth and show me
the simplest of paths to peace.
She will shine in the darkest corners of my mind
with a clear bright light, undimmed by lies.
She will call me to be true to God,

to others' needs before my own,
and to myself.

She will train my eyes to see what's true, what's just,
what's pure: deserving of my will and love.
A demanding and jealous lover,
she will countenance no other claims upon my heart.

Do I dare invite your Wisdom, Lord,
to settle in my soul?
Dwell deeply in my thoughts?
Take hold my heart's desires?
In the stillness of my prayer, Lord,
let Wisdom settle in my soul
and take me as her own. Amen.

THE BROKEN HEART OF JESUS

God of all our hearts,
give us the courage and grace
to look upon the broken heart of our brother, Jesus,
and to find in his heart the forgiveness of our sins.

Help us to break ourselves open, as did he,
in sacrifice and service for our sisters and brothers.
In Jesus' name we pray. Amen.

THE HIDDEN THINGS

Lord,
There's nothing in the world
hidden from your sight.

Sometime today,
give me the will and the courage
to share with you in prayer
even one thing
I've tried to hide from you—
and maybe even from myself. Amen.

WHO WAITS FOR MY FORGIVENESS, LORD?

Your mercy is inexhaustible, Lord:
freely offered and readily given
to all who need it, to any who ask for it.

I know this to be true in my own life,
and I'm grateful for your pardon of my failings.

But who waits for *my* mercy, Lord?
Who waits to be pardoned by me?
Who waits for me to forgive?

Is it someone at home? At work? At school?
Is it a neighbor or someone far away?
Is it someone I don't want to forgive?
Someone I've refused to forgive?
Someone I've judged to be undeserving of my mercy?
Is it someone who has died?

Whoever it might be,
even someone I can't connect with right now:
let this be a day when I forgive others, Lord,
as freely as you've forgiven me. Amen.

Your Lavish Beauty

Sometimes, Lord,
there's an extravagance of lush beauty
growing right outside the window.

Not just one or two but dozens of blossoms,
and each a bouquet of smaller blooms:
beauty, dense and delicate.

Open my eyes to your lavish beauty,
delicate and dense, all around me
and in the lives of all whose paths cross mine.
Amen.

A New Heart

I will give you a new heart and place a new spirit within you,
taking from your bodies your stony hearts
and giving you natural hearts. . . .
You shall be my people and I will be your God.
—Ezekiel 36:27, 26

A new heart sounds like a good idea, Lord!
A new heart that's whole, healed and mended.
A heart that's free of burdens,
a heart no longer haunted by painful memories.
A heart softened by compassion and generosity,
the rough edges of selfishness finally smoothed away.
A heart made light by your mercy and peace,
a heart I'd be proud to open and share with others.

I know I'm yours, Lord,
because I know that all belongs to you.
But I also know that I hold back.
I'm often slow to offer you what truly is your own.

So give me a new heart, Lord,
and help me surrender the stony heart within.

Help me let go what I neither want nor need,
what doesn't nourish or sustain me.
Help my heart to be quiet in the stillness of your presence.

In the silence of my prayer today,
give me a new heart, Lord,
and place a new spirit within me.
Help me to slow down, to be still, to pray,
and to know that you are near, now, today.
Amen.

Feasts and Liturgical Seasons

A Prayer for the Feast of Christ the King

Today we celebrate your kingship, Lord,
even though you told us in so many ways
not to make you a king.

But I just might need a king.

I need you to reign over my life
because, left to my own devices,
I mess things up far too often.

I need you to rule over my passions:
my hungers and my desires too often override
my thinking, my reasoning, and my conscience.

I need you to govern and hold sway
over my erratic ways, my ups and downs,
my inconsistent unpredictability.

I need you to decree again the law of love,
commanding me to give, generously,
when I'm so tempted to hold back.

Be my king, Lord:
reign with loving order over chaos in my day;
rule with gentle strength when I start to go astray;
and govern with your word of truth the way I live my life.

Be my king, Lord,
and rule with gentle grace my heart and soul
and all my thoughts and words and deeds,
that I might serve you always,
loyal to your name. Amen.

A Prayer for Advent

Prepare a way for you, Lord?
I've got lots of work to do!

Help me prepare a way for you into my home, Lord:
help me find a place, a room, a corner, a chair
where you and I can meet each day to pray.
Perhaps I'll put a candle there, with a Bible;
maybe a statue or a picture; a rosary or a prayer card:
something to mark the spot as the place I keep
to go each day to sit and rest, to take a deep breath,
to remember your presence and open my heart in prayer.

Help me prepare a way for you on my calendar,
an "appointment" each day;
even just ten minutes for you and me to get together,
to talk about the day, its ups and downs,
and get to know each other just a little better than yesterday.

Help me prepare a way for you to enter my thoughts, Lord.
When I'm trying to figure things out, nudge me
to ask for your guidance and counsel,
your Spirit and your wisdom,
when I'm making decisions and choices.
Help me prepare a way for you, Lord,
in my family and among my friends, at work and at school,

in my parish and in my neighborhood.
Help me prepare a way for you to come into the hearts
of those around me who are alone.

Help me prepare a way for you, Lord,
in the crazy rush of Christmas all around me.
Help me remember it's *your* birthday
and that you should get some presents—from me.
Help me remember the poverty of your nativity:
make your way into my wallet and spend generously
on those whose needs are so much greater than my own.
Help me remember that of all the gifts I might receive,
none is greater than the love you have for me.

Help me prepare a way for you
to enter my life decisively, Lord.
In the quiet of my prayer, Lord,
help me clear the path you walk into my life, into my soul.

In the stillness of my prayer, Lord,
help me see you as you make your way towards me,
and show me that no matter the roadblocks I put up,
you'll find a way to come, to enter,
and to fill me with your presence. Amen.

A Christmas Prayer

Child of Mary's womb,
apple of Joseph's eye,
welcome us when we come to you:
to visit, to pray,
simply to draw near.

Set our gaze on only that star
whose light leads us
along the path of your truth.

Teach us to make of our hearts
the finest gift we have to offer
to you and to others.

When we wonder if we have found you—
or lost you—
deepen our faith
in your faithful pursuit of us,
our lives, and our love.

Appear, shine, and reveal
the beauty of your face to us,
that we might never fail to see you
in all we meet and know.

Guide us, Lord Jesus,
by your perfect light. Amen.

A Prayer for Epiphany

O Magi,
were you confused?

Did you wonder if you'd taken a left for a right
or misjudged the bright star's GPS?

Was it all a big mistake?
Could this really be the street?
The place?
The door?

The light spills into night
and beckons and calls:
"This way! Come this way!
Let go your thoughts
of what should be or might have been,
and open up to what is here,
to what will be,
to where *he* is and where he dwells
in the light his presence warms
on this chilled and darkened night!"

Teach us your wisdom, Lord:
open our eyes to your star above
and our hearts to your glowing presence
within us, around us,
and living just across the street,
lighting the paths we walk each day,
lifting us up and out of our darkness
to your radiant and holy face. Amen.

A Lenten Prayer

I return to you today, Lord,
with a heart sometimes burdened
by the sins of my past.

Remind me, Lord, that before I sin,
before I even *think* of sinning,
you stand ready to forgive me,
so deep is your desire to be one
with your sons and daughters.

As far as the east is from the west,
so far do you put my sins away from me:
in your goodness, let me know and trust
that you have forgiven and forgotten my sins.

Wipe my sins from my heart, Lord,
the ones I seem unable to forget,
and free me from the sinful ways
I find so hard to leave behind.

Thoroughly wash me of my guilt, Lord;
let no memories haunt and keep me
a prisoner to my own past.

Wash away my guilt and cleanse my heart
of any trace of my past wrongs:
with a heart reconciled and renewed,
refresh me with your grace,
that I might walk again
the path you have set out for me.

In your great compassion, Lord,
forgive my sins and free me
for the love you stand ready
to offer me each day. Amen.

Wash My Soul This Lent

If you, LORD, mark our sins,
Lord, who can stand?
But with you is forgiveness
and so you are revered.
—Psalm 130:3-4

No sin is beyond your mercy, Lord:
your forgiveness is deep and wide,
a river of pardon and peace.

Give me a contrite heart,
that I might know and confess
my failures, my silence, my selfish habits,
my carelessness, my pride, and my faults.

Wash my soul this Lent, Lord,
in the waters of your grace. Amen.

A Prayer for Good Friday

Jesus, we come this night
and gather at the foot of your cross.

Only the promise of your mercy
makes us, sinners,
bold enough to stand before you,
who bore every sin of every one of us
upon your strong and innocent shoulders.

Only the promise of your peace
gives us sinners strength
to look upon your wounds
and blood shed for us,
that we might be saved.

Only the hope of healing
gives us sinners humility
sufficient to gaze upon your body
broken for us,
for the mending of our souls.

Only the gift of your humanity
gives us sinners cause
to hope our fallen flesh

might be redeemed
in the offering of your own.

Only the gift of your divinity
helps us sinners dare
to hope our hearts might
rise at last with yours
into the Father's arms.

Only the infinite depths of your love
give us grace to trust that you,
the innocent Lamb of God,
look with sweet mercy
on sinners such as us.

Jesus, Lamb of God,
save and redeem us,
lift us up out of our sins
and into the embrace of your outstretched arms.

Jesus, Lamb of God,
falsely accused, stripped and beaten,
have mercy on us.

Jesus, Lamb of God,
crowned with thorns, humiliated, crucified,
have mercy on us.

Jesus, Lamb of God,
sacrificed for your beloved people,
have mercy on us.

Jesus, our Passover and our peace,
our Savior and Redeemer,
our exodus from sin, our deliverance from death,
you take away our sins and the sins of the world:
have mercy on us this night
as we gather at the foot of your cross. Amen.

An Easter Prayer

In my corner of the universe
spring waits, about to wake,
ready to rise from still-cold ground
through patches of snow,
warming to the sun in gardens
thirsty for April's rains.

I know that spring will come, Lord:
a blooming green triumph over winter's sway,
with breezes sweeping clean the sidewalks
and paths that lead to summer's rest.

I'm sure that spring will come around me, Lord,
but I pray for a springtime deep within my soul:
a rising up of hope in a winter-chilled heart
through remnants of sin and hurt
to a mind thawed of worried fears,
to a spirit fresh with mercy's morning dew.

I offer you my heart this morning, Lord,
waiting to wake, ready to rise,
to be lifted up by your loving hand.

Rise within me, Lord,
with grace, with mercy and newfound life.
Breathe your Spirit's life within me,
sweeping clean the pathways of my heart.

Spring clean my soul for Easter joy
and resurrect my hope in you,
and in the season of your grace that has no end,
wake the springtime of your life within me.

And make me mindful, Lord, of others,
waking from their own wintry days.
Keep us patient with each other
as we stretch and bud and bloom and
wait for you in all the ways you spring to life
within us and among us.

So my hope and prayer for spring I offer you
this morning, Lord,
and through this week and on until
the peace of Easter rises in my heart. Amen.

A Prayer for Pentecost

Come, Holy Spirit,
and fill my heart again
with the fire and power of your gifts.

Come, Holy Spirit,
and with *wisdom* help me know what's real,
to see through God's own eyes.

Come, Holy Spirit,
and with *understanding* light my way
to follow all that faith reveals.

Come, Holy Spirit,
and be my beacon of *right judgment,*
with counsel prudent, just, and sure.

Come, Holy Spirit,
and kindle in my soul the *courage*
to do what's right, what's true and pure.

Come, Holy Spirit,
and give me *knowledge* of God's plans
for my life, my gifts and talents.

Come, Holy Spirit,
and bend my mind and heart
to *reverence* God above all others.

Come, Holy Spirit,
and in *awe and wonder* stoke my heart's desire
to do always what God asks of me and nothing less.

Come, Holy Spirit,
fill my mind and heart with your light and gifts
and my soul with your breath of peace.

Come, Holy Spirit,
and draw me to the Father's love
through Christ, my Lord and Savior. Amen.

Holidays

A Prayer for New Year's Eve

It's almost New Year's Eve, Lord,
in a year that seemed so very new
not very long ago.

Where has the old year gone, Lord,
and how did I live, how did I spend
these fleeting past twelve months?

I remember the times
we walked and talked together, you and I.

And I remember the times
I forgot, somehow,
that you were right there by my side.

I think of times you took delight in me
and times I failed to live your word
in what I said and did.

And yet you never failed to love me,
to pardon and forgive me, Lord:
your grace so pure and always freely given.

And in return, I come with empty hands:
I haven't much to offer and all I have
was first your gift to me.

But now there comes a new year
and with it comes my prayer
to be more worthy of your love.

In this new year, Lord,
make me stronger in faith
and more trusting in your help.

Nurture in my soul a hunger for the truth,
a thirst for the holy, a desire for wisdom
Help me settle for nothing less
than what comes from your heart, Lord,
to mend and heal my own.

It's almost New Year's Eve,
in a year that seemed so very new
not very long ago.

Wake my heart to this new year, Lord,
and to all your grace and gifts:
let a new day dawn in peace. Amen

God's Valentine to Me

No one has loved you *longer* than I have:
I loved you before you were born or conceived;
I loved you before time began.

No one holds you *closer* than I do:
I'm right by your side 24/7/365;
I'm truly your Best Friend Forever.

No one loves you more *faithfully* than I do:
my love for you is unfailing;
I love you with no strings attached.

No one loves you more *wisely* than I do:
I guide you through all of your troubles;
my wisdom and truth are your peace.

No one loves you more *mercifully* than I do:
I freely forgive you and forgive you again;
I will never walk out or give up on you.

No one loves you more *deeply* than I do:
I dwell in your heart of hearts;
I make my home in the depths of your soul.

No one loves you more *joyfully* than I do:
I delight in the person I made you to be;
I love you more than you know or imagine.

No one loves you more *passionately* than I do:
I gave my Beloved out of love for you;
now I call you my chosen, my child, my own.

No one loves you more *graciously* than I do:
I love you more than anyone has,
more than anyone could or ever will.

No one loves you more *fully* than I do,
for indeed, I Am Love: I abide in you
and you in me, forever and ever. Amen.

A Memorial Day Prayer

You who created us,
who sustain us,
who call us to live in peace,
hear our prayer this day.

Hear our prayer for all who have died,
whose hearts and hopes are known to you alone.

Hear our prayer for those who put the welfare of others
ahead of their own,
and give us hearts as generous as theirs.

Hear our prayer for those who gave their lives
in the service of others,
and accept the gift of their sacrifice.

Help us to shape and make a world
in which we will lay down the arms of war
and turn our swords into ploughshares
for a harvest of justice and peace.

Comfort those who grieve the loss of their loved ones
and let your healing be the hope in our hearts.

Hear our prayer this day,
and in your mercy answer us
in the name of all that is holy. Amen.

A PRAYER FOR THE FOURTH OF JULY

In the spirit of this holiday, I pray:

Keep me hungry for what's real,
independent of my fantasies.
Keep me honest in my speech,
independent of the easy lie.
Keep me obedient to your word,
independent of my stubborn will.
Keep me just in all my dealings,
independent of deceit.
Keep me loyal to what's true,
independent of the counterfeit.
Keep me constant in compassion,
independent of self-interest.

Keep me loyal to my friends,
independent of betrayal.
Keep me strong in self-awareness,
independent of denial.
Keep me humble and forgiving,
independent of conceit.
Keep me positive and hopeful,
independent of my fears.

Keep me faithful in my prayer,
independent of my laziness.
Keep me steadfast in my faith,
independent of my pride.

Make me dependent only
on your love and on your mercy,
on your Spirit and your grace,
all to free my heart to live
independent of all else. Amen.

A Prayer for Labor Day

O God, creator of the world,
of sun and moon and stars,
you chose to fashion us as your own,
your handiwork of love.

Indeed, we are your hands' own work,
and yet into *our* hands
you give the care
of every living thing.

In more ways than we can count,
our work builds up—
or tears apart—
what came as gift from you.

Keep us faithful in preserving
all you've given,
lest we harm the smallest part
of all you've made.

Give us good and honest work to do
and rest at each day's end.
Let a just and fair day's wage be paid
for a good day's work well done.

Give us work that nurtures and sustains
the ones who serve and those they serve.
Let those who labor work in peace,
in freedom, without fear.

Give those in need a job to do,
and to the tired, well-earned rest.
Let all our toil and labor, Lord,
give glory to your name. Amen.

A Prayer for 9/11

Gracious God,
all good gifts come from your hand,
and into our clumsy grasp
you entrust the precious realities
of life, justice, and peace.

We remember this day
how fragile is the gift of peace
and how vulnerable are we
in each other's hands.

We remember those who died
and those who mourn their loss.

We remember those whose courage
gave us a new model for bravery.

We remember those who gave their lives
in their efforts to save others.

We remember that day, that sunny morning,
when the borders of our nation
were broken through to the depths of our hearts.

We remember and we pray
for the healing and peace
that only you can give
and that all of us must share.

Bring us to the day, O God,
when war is but a memory
and peace our way of life.
Bring us to the day, O God,
when the harvest of justice
will nourish the people of all nations.

Hasten the advent of that day, O God,
and let our pride not stand in its way.

We ask this through Christ our Lord. Amen.

A PRAYER FOR VETERANS DAY

God of peace,
we pray for those who have served our nation,
who laid down their lives
to protect and defend our freedom.

We pray for those who have fought,
whose spirits and bodies are scarred by war
and whose nights are haunted by memories
too painful for the light of day.

We pray for those who serve us now,
especially for those in harm's way:
shield them from danger
and bring them home—soon.

Turn the hearts and minds
of our leaders and our enemies
to the work of justice and a harvest of peace.
Spare the poor, Lord, spare the poor!

May the peace you left us,
the peace you gave us,
be the peace that sustains,
the peace that saves us.

Christ Jesus, hear us!
Lord Jesus, hear our prayer! Amen.

A Prayer for Thanksgiving Day

Today I thank you, Lord, for the gift of faith:
that strength, power, and source within
showing me the way,
guiding me in the dark,
making sure my faltering step,
giving light for finding truth
and hope for living gracefully
through trials and troubled times.

Today I thank you, Lord,
for the gift of your Church:
that wounded, ragtag, joyful company of saints and sinners
whose faith is my strength, binding us all together,
brothers and sisters in you and in your love.

Today I thank you, Lord, for all the people around me
and those behind me and before me:
the ones who've helped to make me the person I've become;
those who've loved me
in ways too many to know or to imagine;
those who've loved me
when I've failed to love them in return;
those who've pardoned and forgiven me
with mercy and with grace;
those who've shared their joy with me,

who fill my heart with peace
and who help me trust and know with hope
that you are ever by my side.

And today I thank you, Lord,
for all the people I have yet to meet
but will.

Today I thank you, Lord,
for the mystery of your presence:
in everyone I know and meet;
in the simplest and most ordinary
moments of each day;
and in the stillness, in the quiet
of the time I spend with you in prayer.

Today I praise and thank you, Lord,
for you are my God
from whom all blessings flow. Amen.

An Empty Chair at the Table

This (Thanksgiving/Christmas), Lord,
there's an empty chair at our table,
an ache in our hearts
and tears on our cheeks.

We might shield others from our grief,
but we can't hide it from you.

We pray for (name your loved ones)
whose loving presence we'll miss
at this homecoming time.

Help us remember and tell again
the stories that knit us as one
with the ones we miss so much.

Open our hearts to joyful memories
of the love we shared
with those who've gone before us.

Let the bonds you forged so deep in our hearts
grow stronger yet
in remembering those who've left our side.

Help us pray and trust that those we miss
have a home in your heart

and a place at your table forever,
and that one day we'll be one with them once again.

Teach us to lean on you and on one another
for the strength we need
to walk through these difficult days.

Open our eyes and our hearts
to the healing, warmth, and peace of your presence.

Give us quiet moments with you in prayer,
with our memories and loss,
with our thoughts and tears.

Be with us to console us and hold us in your arms
as you hold the ones we miss.

Even in our grief, Lord,
this is the day that you have made:
help us be glad in the peace you've promised,
the peace we pray you share with those
who've gone before us.

For ourselves, Lord,
and for all who find the holidays to be a difficult time,
we make this prayer. Amen.

the WORD
among us®
The *Spirit* of Catholic Living

This book was published by The Word Among Us. Since 1981, The Word Among Us has been answering the call of the Second Vatican Council to help Catholic laypeople encounter Christ in the Scriptures.

The name of our company comes from the prologue to the Gospel of John and reflects the vision and purpose of all of our publications: to be an instrument of the Spirit, whose desire is to manifest Jesus' presence in and to the children of God. In this way, we hope to contribute to the Church's ongoing mission of proclaiming the gospel to the world so that all people would know the love and mercy of our Lord and grow more deeply in their faith as missionary disciples.

Our monthly devotional magazine, *The Word Among Us*, features meditations on the daily and Sunday Mass readings, and currently reaches more than one million Catholics in North America and another half million Catholics in one hundred countries around the world. Our book division, The Word Among Us Press, publishes numerous books, Bible studies, and pamphlets that help Catholics grow in their faith.

To learn more about who we are and what we publish, log on to our website at www.wau.org. There you will find a variety of Catholic resources that will help you grow in your faith.

Embrace His Word, Listen to God . . .

www.wau.org